the emotional animal

Within a holistic philosophy that focuses on the dog/human relationship, many training methodologies can be happily employed. By its very definition, however, a holistic philosophy must embrace the whole, discarding or cautiously employing techniques which ignore the entire mind/body/soul interconnections which exist for both dog and handler.

The current trend in dog training focuses on the principles and theories of operant conditioning. While certainly an improvement over training techniques which evolved from harshly compulsive war dog training methods, operant conditioning also fails to treat the dog as a whole.

Informed largely by the work of behaviorist B.F. Skinner, operant condition is a relatively dry, scientific approach that ignores emotions. Skinner and his followers believed that only behavior that could be seen objectively could be studied or understood scientifically.

Much of the study of behavior took place within the laboratory setting in highly controlled settings. No less an expert than Konrad Lorenz had this to say about such studies:

body posture & emotions

> *"I have always maintained that in order to get to know a higher form of life, you must live with the animal. The arrogance of today's researchers who believe that they can answer every question by examining an animal experimentally was always foreign to my nature. The truly interesting questions only arise when one has become directly acquainted with animals. One must live in close contact with them . . ."*

Lorenz did indeed live in close contact with the subjects of his studies. And his observations of multiple species remain among the most interesting and informative in the field of animal behavior. Willing to attribute emotional responses to his subjects, his writings are sprinkled with descriptive phrases such as "falling in love," "demoralized," "grieving."

Beyond Skinner came the "cognitive revolution" of the late 1960s, when scientists interested in psychology and behavior focused on the actual workings of the brain to learn and store information. Messy, complex and impossible to quantify, emotions were simply left out of the picture.

Increasingly, psychological sciences focused on a computer like model of the brain: Input X would result in output Y. The reductionist simplicity of this view was perhaps best spoofed in the Gary Larson cartoon featuring two amoebas with one complaining to the other, "*Stimulus, response, stimulus, response.*"

shifting shapes, shifting minds

As Daniel Coleman says so well in his book, **Emotional Intelligence**:

> "The cognitive scientists who embraced this view...[were] forgetting that, in reality, the brain's wetware is awash in a messy, pulsating puddle of neurochemicals, nothing like the sanitized, orderly silicon that has spawned the guiding metaphor for mind."

Even today, with a focus on cognition and evolutionary explanations for observable behavior, comparative psychology gives us interpretations such as "ultimate causation" when an animal chooses a mate, rather than interpreting the pairing in emotional terms, such as Lorenz's "falling in love."

Emotions in animals is a taboo scientific subject, but the times may be changing. For the sake of not only the animals, but for ourselves as compassionate, empathic beings, I certainly hope so.

(For a comprehensive look at the topic, I recommend highly the bestseller **When Elephants Weep** by Jeffrey Masson.)

body posture & emotions

once upon a time, there was a man in the shower...

Once upon a time, my husband was taking a shower. Since he'd been having problems with listening to every precious syllable I utter each day, I decided to "see what he would do." I called him in a happy, clear tone of voice: "John, come here!" I could hear him in the shower, happily soaping his nether regions, and I just knew he was ignoring me. I called again, but still no response.

Obviously, he was deliberately ignoring me. After all, he understood perfectly well what "come here" meant. Why, we'd been over it a thousand times! Well, I'd been warned that he might be hard to train. From the Midwest, he's of Irish descent and has never been neutered. And you know what that means!

I decided to nip any dominance display in the bud, and marched angrily to the bathroom. Reaching past the shower curtain, I grabbed him by the neck and snarled, "I told you to come here!"

Unfortunately, he had soap in his eyes and was singing to himself and hadn't heard me coming. His training as a policeman kicked in, and in three seconds flat he had me

shifting shapes, shifting minds

pinned up against the wall and was frisking me (the only enjoyable part of this whole fiasco!).

Now that I've had a chance to talk to my friends about his unacceptable aggressive behavior, I realize I may have to consider getting rid of him. What do you think?

This is a pretty ludicrous fairy tale, isn't it? But how much would it change your reaction if I went back and changed a few things around and made John a dog busy chewing on a bone instead of taking a shower (though the story might be more mysterious if the dog were showering)? Would I be within my "rights" to not let him get away with that?

"You can't let him get away with that!" seems to be a prevailing war cry in training sessions throughout the country. Implied in that one frantic sentence is a world of doom, of complete abdication of power by a hapless handler, of Machiavellian plots by the dog in question to take over the universe (or at least the house in which he lives), and all sorts of problems any sensible person would take precautions to avoid.

In that one sentence is someone's doctoral dissertation on "*Domestic Animals: A Study of the Fears Created in Authoritarian Controlling Personalities (with High Hostility/Paranoia Index Ratings) by Canine Acts of Non-Compliance with Demands.*"

body posture & emotions

Argue training theory, dominance theory, pack behavior - whatever you will, but it all boils down to this: we have a *relationship* with our dogs. Like any relationship, it is most fulfilling for all involved, most nurturing to the individuals involved and most successful when it is based on mutual respect, understanding, and *reasonable expectations*.

But even deeper is the foundation for any relationship - trust. In the silly fairy tale above, any careful reader would conclude that the fictitious me had some serious issues about trusting John to care about me, listen to me and respond to my needs. Without a basis of trust, each and every one of his actions would be suspect, to be viewed defensively as a challenge. You don't need to be a certified marriage counselor to predict that such a relationship would be troubled.

What is also missing from the above fairy tale is a critical element - John's emotions. While you gather a strong sense of my feelings, there is nothing to indicate that I was even aware of or considered his feelings. For a relationship to be strong and healthy, there needs to be understanding and consideration for the emotions of our partners.

shifting shapes, shifting minds

madness in our methods

Whatever your preferred method, any training approach that fails to include and understand the reality of an animal's emotions is limiting at best. In the book, **When Elephants Weep**, the authors put it more bluntly: *"Training an animal will meet with little success if the trainer has no insights into the animal's feelings."*

To deny an animal's emotions is to distance yourself from him as a feeling being. For centuries on end, this distance has allowed humanity to commit some terrible acts on beings considered inferior, which at times have included human babies, other races, and of course, animals. It is much easier to impose your will, through whatever means, on another creature whose emotional state can be denied.

Although we talk of loving our dogs, and indeed, spend endless amounts of time and energy on their behalf, a contradiction remains between our feelings and our actions. One of the better selling books that purports to assist the reader in becoming their dog's "best friend" talks in glowing language of the dog/human connection. Yet just a few pages later, you find this advice regarding physical discipline:

body posture & emotions

"How hard do you hit the dog? A good general rule is that if you did not get a response, a yelp or other sign, after the first hit, it wasn't hard enough."

Thus, despite our great love for our dogs, barbaric training methods (especially those wrapped in beautiful philosophies) remain in vogue, largely unquestioned or challenged.

Those who do raise questions about training methods are dismissed as bleeding hearts and/or unknowledgeable in the ways of dogs. But I am not talking about the pet owner who considers it cruel to put her dangerously obese dog on a diet. I don't mean the well meaning but misinformed owner who gives a young puppy the run of the house because confining the puppy for its own safety is "unnatural."

I am talking about commonplace, widely accepted practices like the use of force and shock collars used to teach basic exercises and ear pinches to teach a retrieve. I'm talking about techniques that you could find without going further than your neighborhood training school or the local obedience match.

Would we tolerate someone training one of our children in this manner? For most people, the answer is absolutely not. To see a beloved child's face fill with confusion, pain and betrayal in the name of training would stop most intelligent humans in their tracks. Yet we disregard the dog's emotional state, justify our actions using pack/dominance theories, and

shifting shapes, shifting minds

cloaking our acts in behavioral terms of stimulus, reinforcement, etc. Ultimately, it appears, the end justifies the means.

There is an old saying *"Where knowledge ends, violence begins."* For many trainers, there is a growing sense of frustration with barbaric methods. They feel the need for a trusting relationship with a dog much more than they feel the need to cover a wall with ribbons, title certificates and trophies. For these thinking and feeling trainers, this booklet was written.

Part of a holistic philosophy is a willingness to learn, in increasingly detail, how and why your dog operates as he does. From study of wolf behavior to anatomy and physiology, the intelligent trainer seeks, in an ever widening circle, new information that may add another piece to the puzzle.

Sometimes, understanding the particulars of why something occurs enlarges the possibilities of how you will choose to respond to it. With knowledge comes true power, which in turn carries with it forbearance, mercy and benevolence.

body posture & emotions

elementary, my dear watson

Understanding, analyzing and resolving behavior, emotions and body language requires a good deal of detective work. As the famous Sherlock Holmes knew, no detail, however small, is insignificant. The more acutely you are able to observe the dog, the more accurate your analysis will be. Acute observation and attention to detail is the hallmark not only of great detectives, but of great trainers.

One of my most bemusing moments as a trainer came when I was working with a dog who had bitten several people. As I worked the dog over a variety of obstacles, his owner commented several times, "I can't believe he hasn't bitten you yet!" I never could decide if she was simply amazed or just disappointed. I wasn't bitten because I watched the dog for even the smallest sign that he was *beginning* to feel threatened.

With this dog, subtle changes in his breathing pattern, the compression of his lips and a constriction of his pupils gave me the only clues I needed. At that point, with no further clues and without pushing until I saw more dramatic signs, it was a simple matter to shift our activity to something less threatening and allow the dog to calm down.

shifting shapes, shifting minds

Ignoring these clear but subtle signs would have undoubtedly caused the behavior to escalate until perhaps we had a full blown aggressive episode ending in a bite. (This dog went on to become a wonderful companion who easily earned his CGC certificate, and a snapshot of him in Santa's lap at a "Photo With Santa" fund raiser remains my favorite of him.)

Dogs live and act in a world of exquisitely subtle signals in their interactions with each other. Our observations and communications in our interactions with them must seem unbelievably coarse at times to these sophisticates of non-verbal communication. Turned around the other way, we would perceive such inattentiveness to our subtle signals as rude, uncaring or perhaps simply stupid.

Our responsibility as handlers and trainers is to attempt to be as skilled in our observations and non-verbal communications with our dogs as they are in their interactions with us.

Learning to become skilled as an observer requires that you practice these skills. As the artist Frederick Franck said in **The Art of Seeing**, *"We often look, but we rarely see."*

Information gathered through careful observation is crucial. Without such information, you cannot make any informed decisions on the dog's behalf. Take the time to observe your dog carefully and often. Like us, dogs change, have off days, and get confused. If you are observant about your dog's body

body posture & emotions

posture and what it tells you about his emotional state, you can make informed decisions.

Assumptions about a dog's understanding or capabilities, unless confirmed by careful observation of the dog himself, can lead to training problems, undermine or destroy your relationship with the dog, and in some cases, are tantamount to cruelty.

For example, at a certain level of knowledge, any growl, snap or threat by the dog is perceived as "aggression" and perhaps even labeled as vicious. A more knowledgeable observer may note that the dog is simply scared and/or defensive, a completely different set of circumstances requiring an alternate solution.

Without knowledge, it is quite likely that the scared dog will be treated in exactly the same manner as a dog who is quite confidently challenging authority. Without knowledge, that treatment could exacerbate the original problem; ultimately, it is the dog who pays the price for our lack of knowledge about him.

shifting shapes, shifting minds

can't let him get away with what?

A favorite client brought me one of her dogs for evaluation. This client is a loving, conscientious dog owner who takes excellent care of her dogs, and spends considerable time and money to learn all that she can about dogs. She had adopted Sam, a toy breed, not quite a year previous, and I thought he was a charming dog well suited to her and her household.

Settling into my chair for the session, I was startled when she began by asking whether I thought Sam should be put to sleep for his aggressive behavior. *What aggressive behavior?* I wondered, watching the sweet little dog Papillon who waited patiently on a chair for our attention.

The story she relayed was not much different from my shower story. Sam was in the kitchen with her husband as he made breakfast. Upstairs, dressing, she decided she should call Sam - just to "see what he would do." Whether Sam heard her or not could not be determined; nonetheless, she called him again with equal results - no response. Now angry, she stomped downstairs and into the kitchen to "reinforce the command."

Seeing her coming, and quite certain that her intent was not to butter some toast for him, Sam panicked. Swooping down

body _posture_ & _emotions_

upon him, she reached for his collar. Sam promptly bit her and ran.

While biting is not an acceptable behavior, it is at times certainly understandable. (Actually, I marvel constantly that more dogs don't bite more people - God knows they are quite often deserving!) Treated in the same fashion, we too might lash out, using our own particular brand of retaliation.

Was Sam dangerously aggressive, unpredictable, in need of euthanasia? No, he was simply scared, confused and defending himself. And his background of previous abuse made his actions all the more understandable.

"But, I can't let him get away with that!" she spluttered indignantly as I explained the situation as it probably appeared from Sam's point of view.

Looking over at Sam, I asked her to carefully describe for me what emotional state she saw at that very moment in his body posture. Clearly and accurately, she described a dog who was patiently waiting even though a little excited about being the sole focus of our attention. He was, she reported, calm, relaxed and happy. I agreed completely with that interpretation. She knew her dog.

I then asked her to describe what Sam had been like when she stormed into the kitchen that fateful morning. What was

shifting shapes, shifting minds

his body posture like? What did she think his emotional state had been?

She told me how Sam had first been startled, then confused and scared, ultimately to the point where he felt it necessary to defend himself. She described a terrified dog, backing away, crouching defensively with ears laid back and tail tucked.

"All right then, finish this sentence for me using an accurate description of what you saw in Sam that morning: *'I can't let him get away with --'*"

"Being scared and confused," she finished glumly, looking at her loving little dog.

"No, you couldn't possibly let him get away with *that!*" And hearing our laughter, the "aggressive" Sam danced in his chair with shining eyes and a happily wagging tail.

With that simple exercise of finishing an all too familiar phrase with an accurate description of the dog's behavior and state of mind as evidenced in his body posture and actions, Sam's owner was able to let go of that particular stumbling block in her relationship with a wonderful little dog.

Even in a fairy tale, calling a man from the shower as a display of my control of him would be considered, by most people, highly unreasonable. Most readers would expect that

body posture & emotions

he would be quite understandably annoyed if not downright angry with a such senseless demand. (To call a man from the shower because the living room was in flames or the FBI was at the door *would* be reasonable.) Equally so, exercising your authority over the dog for the sheer sake of doing so, as Sam's owner did that fateful morning, is not reasonable in my opinion. Yet owners do it again and again.

Treat your dog like the friend that he is. Weighing in the cultural differences which require you to act more precisely and consistently than you might need to with a human friend (canine culture is a more precise and polite one), there is still a great deal of latitude for a reasonable relationship. Being a clear, fair leadership figure for your dog does not mean becoming a dictator.

If you find yourself muttering, "I can't let him get away with that!" remember that the sentence doesn't end there. Fill in the blanks with an accurate description of the dog's response, and you may find all the answer you need.

Be fair, be reasonable, and above all, never call a dog who's in the shower.

shifting shapes, shifting minds

what you see is what you get

There are powerful correlations between body posture, breathing patterns, facial expressions and emotional states. Most people have an intuitive understanding of these correlations. For example, if faced with an hysterical child, what would you do? Most of us would encourage the child to "sit down, calm down and take some deep breaths." In most cases, this approach would be very effective.

What you may not realize is that when you encouraged the child to sit down and calm down, you were also encouraging a positive shift in his physiological state. This is what body language is all about - the *outward* expression of *internal* physiological states.

Dr. Ian Dunbar has long recognized the value of specific postures as aggression prevention. Teaching a dog to play bow or to roll over and present his belly for a good scratch not only amuses those people the dog meets, but it actually positions the dog so that an aggressive response is highly unlikely. (An additional bonus is that, depending on the breed, such non-aggressive postures from the dog reduces the human anxiety about meeting a "Turn-On-U-Hund".)

Thanks to unfailing animal honesty, the outward expression of relaxation or playful invitation will not be matched by an

body _posture_ & _emotions_

internal state of aggression. Only humans (and some of the higher primates) are capable of smiling and stabbing you simultaneously! With a dog, what you see is what you get.

Affecting emotional states through a change of body posture is so simple that people are often unwilling to believe it. Recently, I had a client with a miniature Dachshund who was very fearful when approached by strangers, an perfectly understandable response from a small dog whose view is of a world largely inhabited by giants' feet.

Loving, playful and even downright playful with the few people she trusted, this little dog adored working and considered obedience and agility training classes an absolute treat. The stand for exam in Novice had been a nightmare that she ultimately passed. But when approached for measurement for her Open jumps, the dog sank back fearfully and mentally, went "bye-bye" for a considerable period after the horror had passed.

Her owner was torn between the dog's apparent enjoyment of any work set before her, and the obvious fear she displayed in certain situations. How could she help her dog get through this? Or, she said sadly, perhaps she should just give up. Several trainers had told her that the problem was genetic and thus unchangeable. While I listened to the history, I watched this little dog carefully for an accurate picture of who she was.

shifting shapes, shifting minds

Reserved, cautious, she was nonetheless a delightful creature whose intelligence and sense of humor gleamed in her eyes. Her normal body posture was not one of a fearful dog, but relaxed. She was not swaggeringly confident, but she did not cower or hide behind her owner's chair. Instead, she happily explored the area around us as we talked.

Her "problem" was apparent only in her response to my overtures, and when the dreaded measuring stick appeared. "Do you see what I mean?" asked the owner in dismay. "What can you do with a response like that?"

"Change the body posture to a more comfortable, productive and relaxed posture, and you will change her emotional state." Based on the owner's expression, I could see my answer was not a sensible (or at least comprehensible) one.

Abandoning words, I set about shifting the body and mind of the dog. In my mind, I held a clear image of this dog in a relaxed body posture. With my hands, I literally began to shape the dog towards that posture. The classic fearful posture of tucked tail, tightened and lowered hindquarters, overall lowered body position and averted head gradually gave way to a tentative stand under my gentle but insistent stroking upwards.

I rubbed her belly to encourage her to stand, breathe and lift her back. With a light touch, I stroked and lifted her head, working on the tight lips and folded ears with some massage

body posture & emotions

to help them loosen up. Since she was motivated by food, I used hot dogs to encourage her to try the unfamiliar posture (at least unfamiliar in that situation) that I was shaping.

The look in her eyes began to shift from sheer frozen panic to a soft, relaxed look. Her breathing, which had all but stopped, became more regular. Her lips, compressed and drawn back, relaxed and her whisker came forward a few degrees. Now standing, her balance, which had shifted backwards, came forward and normalized. Her head and eye movements became slow, thoughtful, normal.

And with all these changes came another change - a willingness to entertain the presence of the measuring stick. Although she still cast a wary eye at the "monster," she seemed almost surprised to discover that when you stand up, breathe, relax and have a hot dog slice or two, it's not so hard to deal with monsters after all.

In less than five minutes, the dog who had bolted in wild eyed panic at the sight of the measuring stick was happily wriggling under the stick which we had shaped into a tunnel. We made our "tunnel" even smaller, and she squashed as much of herself through it as she could without a care in the world that she was now draped in the dreaded stick. The owner's comment? "But that's so simple!" And it is.

shifting shapes, shifting minds

reactions - fight or flee?

I always find it amusing when an owner informs me that their dogs is "dominant" or "submissive." Unfailingly, I ask, "All the time?" And inevitably, the answer is yes, all the time. This obviously cannot be true - for a dog to spend his entire day in a dominant or submissive posture, he would have a very hard time getting a drink, taking a nap, going for a walk, eating a meal or playing with his toys.

What the owner means to say is that in a situation that the dog perceives as confrontational, he has a characteristic reaction. The dominant dog responds in one way, the submissive dog in another. Simply put, if given an option, will the dog resort to fight or flight?

These reactive postures are not the norm for any dog. For the most part, your dog spends his days in a fairly relaxed, neutral state of mind which shifts only as a *reaction* to events.

How would you go about evaluating toward which end of the submissive/dominant spectrum a dog might lean? Watching him alone in the backyard or run would tell you very little. You would learn much more by setting up a situation, such as a stranger entering the yard or run, or a dog outside the fence, or someone trying to take his food or toys from him.

body posture & emotions

The purpose of such tests would be to determine the dog's *reactions*. Does he flee? Does he flight? Does his reaction fall somewhere in between, or depend on the situation?

A reaction is an alteration in the state of being. The dictionary defines reaction as: *"bodily response to or activity aroused by a stimulus; mental or emotional disorder forming an individual's response to his life situation."*

A dog who is sitting calmly is in a different state of being than a dog who is cowering, or standing stiffly with head up and tail held still. Both submissive or dominant postures reflect a *reactive* state - the dog cannot learn effectively, if at all, at such a time, no more than you could be a good student if forced into a violent confrontation with your teacher or cowering fearfully at his feet.

There is a considerable difference between a dog who is deliberately and thoughtfully disregarding a handler's command or actions, and the dog who is stressed and in a flight or fight *reaction*. This distinction between a *reaction* and a *thoughtful response* is an extremely important one.

Most people are familiar with the fight-or-flight response, which is triggered by stress or any *perceived* threat. This physiological *reaction* serves as a protective mechanism, automatically preparing the body, through an extremely rapid and complex process of neurochemical adaptations, to either fight or flee a threatening situation.

The reaction can also be expressed by the animal "freezing" or literally fainting (fortunately a rare phenomena, and technically a different neurochemical response). While most of us can recognize an animal prepared to run away or fight, the *freeze* response is often misunderstood as stubbornness or an outright refusal by the animal to perform as desired.

When an animal reacts by freezing, the muscles are tensed, the breath is held or extremely shallow, and the animal is, momentarily, *literally* unable to move. If forced, the animal may explode into fighting, or run away if the opportunity arises. Using physical force, whether a harsh correction or simply touching the collar, may also cause the animal to become overwhelmed and over stressed.

Reactions by the animal should be accepted by the trainer as just that - involuntary reactions and *not* deliberate actions. A dog who growls when nervous, for example, is often reacting and not thinking. To "correct" a dog for this reaction is not only meaningless, but often intensifies the dog's fear - he would have fled the situation given the opportunity.

This common failure to understand and appreciate the difference between a reaction and a deliberate action usually results in the use of increased force as the trainer attempts to force the animal to "submit" to him. This can create a vicious cycle of fearfulness on the dog's part, use of force, increased fear, and so on, until a habitual reaction is established.

body posture & emotions

A typical example is the dog who lunges, barks and growls at other dogs because, lacking social experience, he is uncertain what else to do. Quite possibly, he also acts this way because his handler has inadvertently reinforced the defensive aggression display through her own body posture and leash cues which intensify the dog's response.

If this dog's reaction is flatly labeled aggression and forcibly "corrected" without observation and understanding of what his body postures reveal about his behavior, his fear will not be resolved, but will intensify.

If his growling is more accurately observed as a fearful reaction, techniques can be used to decrease his fear and allow him to learn more comfortable ways of socializing with other dogs.

Beyond the outward expression of an internal state, there are complex physiological changes at work within your dog's body. Let's take a closer look at exactly how these neurochemical reactions influence your dog's emotions, and how you can use this knowledge to positively influence his emotional state.

shifting shapes, shifting minds

can't think straight

Within the brain are two areas which dog trainers should understand - the *limbic system* which is responsible for strong emotions, and the *prefrontal cortex* which is responsible for the attention to a given task or problem.

In the complicated circuitry of the brain, scientists have discovered an inverse relationship between activation of the cortex and activation of the limbic system. *When one is activated, the other is inhibited.* A dog or person who is in the grips of a strong emotion (i.e., the fight or flight response is activated) *literally* cannot think straight. This is not necessarily a conscious choice, but a neurochemical reality.

anatomy of an emotion

When dealing with the fight portion of the reaction, more commonly labeled "aggression" in animals and "anger/rage" in humans, findings from new research into emotions and the workings of the brain offer some interesting insight on the neurochemistry of this particular emotion.

According to University of Alabama psychologist Dolf Zillman,

body posture & emotions

> *"a universal trigger for anger is the sense of being endangered. Endangerment can be signaled not just be an outright physical threat but also, as is more often the case, by a symbolic threat to self-esteem or dignity; being treated unjustly or rudely, being insulted or demeaned, being frustrated in pursuing an important goal."*

My experience leads me to view the above list as completely applicable to dogs as well as people. Both species are social animals, and within social structures dignity, self-esteem, injustice, rudeness, insults and frustrations play important roles in the lives of individual society members.

Stress of all descriptions can lower the threshold for what provokes anger. A dog who is not feeling well may be quicker to snarl at a rude puppy; a handler who has had a hard day at the office may be faster to take a dog's mistake as an insult.

Beyond the immediate hormonal changes of flight or fight, anger has more lasting effects. A generalized state of "action readiness" can last *hours*, and *subsequent reactions can be triggered faster*. In the case of the "aggressive" dog who is treated with counter-aggression (also known as training techniques), the results can be disastrous.

shifting shapes, shifting minds

According to Zillman's research, when the body is already is in a state of "action readiness" emotions subsequently triggered are of especially great intensity. Thus a dog who might have offered nothing more than a warning growl may respond to a "correction" with an snap, which in turn is treated with more force, which in turn may lead to the dog actually exploding in an outright attack. A dog who is anxious may escalate, if pushed, to a full blown panic attack.

Zillman notes that one of the first scientific studies on anger (done in 1899) offers a highly effective way of de-escalating anger: *"cooling off physiologically by waiting out the adrenal surge in a setting where there are not likely to be further triggers for rage."* This may also be reasonable advice for dealing with the adrenal surges created by fear.

Other approaches useful for changing the body's physiology to a lower degree of arousal: relaxation methods (including changes in breathing and muscle relaxation), distraction through *enjoyable* activities, and active exercise.

sorry, I wasn't listening

The recommendation of distraction through enjoyable activities as a way to alter physiology sends us back to the beginning of this section where we learned that activation of the "thinking" portion of the brain had an inhibitory effect on the limbic system. A dog or person who is focused on a task

body   posture   &   emotions

is not easily overwhelmed by powerful emotions. In fact, they may tune out stimuli not relevant to the task. This is why even dogs that loathe each other are often able to work peacefully side by side - their focus is not on their emotional responses to each other but on their task. (Of course, in their leisure hours...)

Despite the "one command, and one command only" notion, the plain truth is that dogs, just like people, often have legitimate reasons for *not* responding to their owner's every command. They may be busy with something that interests them, and a strong focus on an activity can create some astounding changes within the brain.

An experiment done with cats used electrodes on the scalp to record brain waves changes when the cat heard a tone. Tone - brain blip, tone - brain blip and so on. But when experimenters put a mouse outside the cat's cage, out of reach but visible, the cat's concentration on the mouse was so extreme that it not only visibly ignored the tone, *but the brain failed to register that any sound had even occurred.*

I'm sure most, if not all, readers have had the experience of being so engrossed in a task that they did not hear/see/smell or feel stimuli outside a narrow focus. Thus, cakes burn and questions may go unanswered while you toil away at something. Not sure? Think about the last time you were in the obedience ring. Tell me about the people outside the

shifting shapes, shifting minds

ring, and what the loudspeaker was babbling during your performance. What people? What loudspeaker?

What we *respect* as total concentration in another human being may be all too quickly viewed as a *challenge* to our authority when displayed by a dog. This springs, in part, from a rather strange conviction that we have control and dominion over animals, and therefore the right to some sort of dictatorship and unfailing attentiveness from our dogs.

I am not saying that a dog should not learn to respond promptly to a given command. I am saying that within the context of a trusting, loving relationship, reasonable expectations are usually met with reasonable response. If not, there's good reason - some of which may be found by spending some time in front of the mirror.

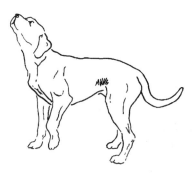

body posture & emotions

shifting shapes, shifting minds

Strong emotions and the ability to think clearly and learn mix about as well as oil and water. For successful training, it is necessary to move both handler and dog from a highly emotional state into a calm, focused and attentive state. As anyone who's had to deal with an upset child, client, co-worker, spouse or animal knows, there's no point in expecting the excited party to communicate clearly, listen calmly or learn anything.

How, then, do we move the dog into a state of mind where learning is not only possible, but facilitated? The first step is to examine your own practices before you set about changing your dog's behavior. While it's easy to focus on the dog's behavior, the unpleasant truth is that the dog may be reacting quite honestly to *our* actions. If we are the source of the problem, then it behooves us to change our behavior before we attempt to assist the dog.

It is beyond the scope of this humble booklet to begin to list the methods employed in the name of training and the ways in which these methods trigger the very reactions and emotional states in the dog that interfere with the learning process. Suffice it to say that any method which incorporates fear, confusion, or aggression from the handler is not

shifting shapes, shifting minds

conducive to learning, curiosity, enjoyment, trust and cooperation.

Sooner or later, every handler encounters a situation with a dog where they must deal with an emotional state and a body posture that needs to be shifted. Whether the undesirable state is due to the dog's natural tendencies to react in certain ways, previous training/handling, past experiences, etc., the history of the problem is unimportant. While understanding the source of a problem is helpful, it does not change the need to do something about it.

I often tell handlers who are in search of detailed explanations of why their dog does X, Y, or Z to pretend that this is a dog they found wandering on the street. This is now an unfamiliar dog they have no prior knowledge of, and the dog's history is a complete unknown. They have nothing more to go on than the absolute here and now.

How will they deal with such a dog? By doing the only thing they can do - observe what the dog's body posture tells them. Is he afraid of them, an object, a situation? How do they know? Is he threatening to bite? Why? What can they do to defuse the aggression?

Given that new perspective, handlers learn to stop overanalyzing why their dog does something, and focus instead on concrete ways to shift the dog's behavior. And then I give them the most powerful training tool of all - an

body posture & emotions

understanding of the correlation between body posture and emotion.

If, by shifting body posture, you can begin to influence and alter the physiological and emotional states, then resolving many behavior problems becomes a relatively straightforward matter. You simply need to answer these two questions:

✵ **What body posture/emotional state would be preferable in any given situation?**

✵ **How will you shape the dog toward that preferred posture and state of mind?**

In any situation, the goal is a return to a neutral, balanced and relaxed state of being where the dog is most capable of learning. It sounds simple, and it is. Remember the Dachshund owner's comment?

There are only a few guidelines for using the *Shifting Shapes, Shifting Minds* approach:

❖ **Accurate observation of the dog when he is not reacting**

Sit back and watch the dog when he is under no pressure or command. If the dog has been brought to your facility, you

shifting shapes, shifting minds

may need to turn him loose for 15 or more minutes before you get a glimpse of his non-reactive body postures. If you have the luxury of watching the dog in his own, familiar environment, this will obviously take less time, but don't forget that your presence may influence the dog.

❖ **Accurate observation of the dog's reactive body posture and emotional state during the situation**

This may be the dog working on a specific exercise, or meeting tall people wearing glasses, or whatever. Listen to what the owner has to say, but give the greatest weight to and believe what the **dog** has to tell you.

More than once I've had clients describe their dog's behavior in ways that made me think Stephen King had interviewed their pet before writing **Cujo**. Face to face with the dog himself, I saw a completely different picture.

The client's description is a truthful one - from *their perspective*, the behavior really is frightening, mysterious or upsetting. Whether you agree with their assessment or not, their *feelings* about the behavior are valid. As a trainer, the client's perceptions are a part of the puzzle that you must deal separately from the dog's behavior.

33

body posture & emotions

❖ **Make a detailed list of the changes in body posture that occur when the dog is stressed or challenged**

Here is where you'll need your observation skills. While tails, ears and overall body position are clues that even a rank novice can learn to read, you will be most effective if you can intervene at the *earliest* signs that the dog has begun to shift from neutral.

This means paying close attention to breathing, shifts in balance and muscular tension, changes in the shape of the eye (including pupil dilation/constriction) as well as the speed and direction of the eye movements, flares of the nostrils and changes in whiskers. All of these signals occur long before the much cruder tail/head/body changes are seen.

❖ **Shift body posture towards normal, relaxed posture**

Changing the posture of the dog can be done in a number of ways - using your hands to guide, stroke, soften, lift, encourage, etc. Unlike the inadvertent reward of petting accompanied by verbal reassurance often giving by well meaning but misinformed owners, the use of the hands in this situation is purposeful and used specifically to change posture, not to soothe or reinforce behavior.

shifting shapes, shifting minds

The sit is my position of choice. Neutral, it neither requires the dog to be in a submissive posture nor allows him to remain in the posture of greater arousal - the stand.

As a rule I do NOT recommend the use of the down as a postural shift, primarily because the times in which you will want to help the dog shift his posture are most often times of great arousal or excitement for the dog. Far too often, I see handlers struggling with dogs, attempting to force them into a down with increasingly violent leash or collar checks, which in turn does nothing to calm the dog but usually does escalate his emotional state. Without much effort, this can turn into a battle in which nothing is accomplished and the owner may be bitten. The same dog, quietly guided into a sit, will usually comply, even if grudgingly.

For a dog who is going the other way, i.e., heading towards a very submissive posture, I will ask for a sit or, occasionally, a stand. When dealing with a dog who is fearful and anxious, these postures help shift the dog to a more confident state. Gently stroke the belly to lift the back, encourage the head to rise above the level of the withers, and using hand or wand, *stroke* (do not force!) the tail up to a neutral position.

Food can be useful to lure and encourage, but be extremely careful. Food is perceived by the dog as a reward, so treats delivered at the wrong time (i.e., when the dog is exhibiting the body posture you don't want) can inadvertently reinforce that posture. This is why the old "approach and offer a treat"

body posture & emotions

technique is fairly useless for timid or fearful dogs. Torn between the food and the fear of approaching someone, these dogs often stretch themselves forward, straining to get the food, but still in the crouched, backwards posture. When they do grab the food, they immediately retreat - in the same posture.

Dr. Ian Dunbar's "treat-retreat" approach carries a double effect and is far more successful. In this approach, a food treat is tossed toward the dog from a distance where the dog shows awareness of the person tossing the food but not a change in posture. The food is thrown so that it lands several feet from the dog, between dog and the thrower. Naturally, to get the treat, the dog must stand up and walk towards it.

Since the person who threw the treat is outside the "reaction zone," the body posture may be hesitant but not extreme as the dog moves forward. Here's the critical detail: *As the dog approaches the food, the person backs away.* The beauty of this approach is that not only is the dog rewarded for coming forward voluntarily, but he also receives another reward: the reduction of social pressure - the scary person moves away.

This technique builds the dog's confidence quickly, which is reflected in his body posture, which builds more confidence, and so on. Ultimately, this approach develops a dog who confidently and voluntarily walks up to strangers in search of treats. (Of course, you now have a new problem in the form of a social pest, but what a nice problem to deal with!)

shifting shapes, shifting minds

offering options

You cannot *force* a dog to change. Certain behaviors are too powerfully rewarding to the dog to be amenable to alteration. You will not, through postural shifts, convince a herding dog not to herd, a bird dog not to hunt, a guard dog not to guard.

You can't tell a fearful dog to act brave, or tell an aggressive dog to back off. But you can offer the dog new behavioral options. The dog is unable to create new options for himself. If frightened by a situation, he cannot tell himself to "stand up straight, take a deep breath and smile." Although that is great advice that would actually work to change his perception and experience of the situation, it falls on deaf ears when it is directed to a dog.

But, by teaching him self control (see my booklet, *Understanding & Teaching Self Control*), you can convince the herding dog to sit quietly until it's his turn in the herding arena instead of leaping about and screaming in frustration. You can keep your bird dog sitting calmly while you organize your equipment. You can help the guarding dog learn that a full blown charge at the door when Aunt Tillie knocks is not your idea of a really cool response.

You can help the fearful dog learn that instead of bolting to the end of the lead they can sit without panicking. The

body posture & emotions

aggressive dog can learn to lengthen his fuse, so that he is less likely to be triggered into unpleasant behavior.

Teaching self control puts limits on impulses and reactions. Not incidentally, teaching a dog self control includes shifting body posture and thus emotional state. Whether headed up the scale or sliding fearfully down it, a shift of body posture can help a dog find that lovely middle ground - a place that is not as maddening or scary, a place where he can think.

It is the trainer's responsibility to be aware of the shifts that take a dog away from the "learning zone" of relaxation, curiosity, trust and enjoyment. And it is the trainer's job to find a way to show the dog how new body postures can create a new experience of any situation. It may sound odd, but the dog is unable to imagine other reactions, other experiences and other outcomes - he literally does not know that he has alternatives.

By and large, the dog has one important advantage over his handler: he has no shame, no guilt, no need to hang on to behaviors that are uncomfortable or non-productive. Presented with a more pleasant, comfortable alternative, the dog will nearly always choose that over the unpleasantness of fear or aggression.

shifting shapes, shifting minds

conclusion

Amidst the complexity of canine behavior, body language, emotions and our relationships with our dogs lies a golden gift. It is a gift bestowed by dogs on even the most inept of handlers, even the most uninformed owner. It is a gift that a wise trainer embraces and carries with him. In acknowledging this gift in every interaction, a wise trainer insures that he will be able, with clarity, love and trust, hear what the dog has to tell him.

The golden gift is this: Intimately connected with his own emotions, the dog cannot lie. What he feels, he expresses. What he shows in his body posture is true, without guile, completely and utterly honest.

Distanced from our own feelings, bound by our fears, we treasure and are amazed by this quality of complete truth in our dogs. If only we were able to share that state of being. Perhaps, in learning to shift shapes and shift minds in our dogs, we also begin our own shifts.